# L I F E

## AFTER
## SURVIVAL

*A Therapeutic
Approach for
Adult Children
of Alcoholics*

PATRICIA A. MANSMANN
PATRICIA A. NEUHAUSEL

For additional information
from authors write to
publishing company
™ Genesis Publishing Company
Box #228
Malvern, Pennsylvania 19355

Cover Design by Karen E. Thorpe

Library of Congress Catalog Card number: 89-080012
ISBN: 0-940967-01-4

Printed in the United States

# Life After Survival

# CONTENTS

# PREFACE

We have written this book in order to share our ideas with other therapists and, we hope, to help them with the difficult job of treating the adult children of alcoholics.

We hope it will provide the kind of clear, concise approach to therapy we were seeking ourselves in our readings and in the many workshops we went to over the years.

In all those workshops, we learned significant information to use in therapy, but we still felt a lack of the kind of structure that both the client and the therapist need. It wasn't until we read Herbert Gravitz and Julie Bowden's work concerning the stages of recovery that we were able to give our approach a more coherent form.

It is our hope that the structure provided here will lighten your load, as it has ours. This book presumes the therapist has a full awareness and knowledge of the adult child syndrome and its symptoms and roles. Many of the books listed in the Suggested Readings provide such needed information.

As you read this book, you will note it makes use of the stages of recovery identified by Gravitz and Bowden. It is important to recognize that although these stages are identified as being separate, they often overlap. We have found that clients may be in one stage on a certain issue and in a different stage on another issue, and may relapse in one area while progressing in others. Therefore, it is important for the therapist to continually observe the client as a total person (even though working on a particular issue) as s/he and her/his issues transform from stage to stage during recovery.

Much energy is being spent by many people around the country on the adult child syndrome. It has been very exciting to us to see how the "springboard effect" of this energy has created such positive momentum in work with adult children. A real spirit of sharing from everyone has moved the field forward in a very fast and exciting pace.

We have found everyone to be very helpful, hopeful and willing to share their work. We are particularly grateful to those who permitted parts of their work to be included in this book. We hope our efforts create another link to all the sharing our predecessors have done.

We would like to acknowledge the following for all their energy and help:

Julie Bowden              John Jones
Marianne Bradley          Phyllis Marron
Paul Curtin               Nick Neuhausel
John Friel                Sharon Wegscheider-Cruse
Herb Gravitz

Credits:
Pat and Ed Krimmel, Consultants
Karen E. Thorpe, Artist
Deborah Lyons, Editorial Consultant

# PREFACE TO SECOND EDITION

Almost two years have passed since the first edition of this book was published. It seems like a much longer time given the amount the ACOA movement (as well as our own practice) has grown and progressed. Like a typical ACOA, the nationwide movement seems to have moved from the emergent awareness stage and to be starting to work on core issues. Similarly, our individual practice seems to have moved from "feeling our way" and "experimenting" to formulating many of our ideas.

The second edition of *Life After Survival*, we hope, will show what two more years in the ACOA field has produced. We feel the methods we have developed have been beneficial to many types of clients, and so we would like to share those ideas with others in the field.

Since we first jotted down an outline of our therapeutic method for working with ACOAs two years ago, we have been so busy experimenting with new and old methods that it has taken us until now to expand that outline. In doing so, we are fulfilling a longstanding intention of sharing more specific techniques with the ACOA community and thereby continuing a dialogue with other ACOA therapists across the country. We hope this second edition will encourage others to share in print the therapeutic techniques that have been useful for them. We are excited to share with all of you in the ACOA network the special insights we have received from our clients as we have watched them becoming more spiritual, "more healthy" and thus more creative as their therapy has progressed. It has been and continues to be a privilege to share their journeys with them.

# FOREWORDS TO SECOND EDITION

There is a social movement numbering in the tens of millions of children of all ages from alcoholic and otherwise traumatic families. Posing a challenge to all health professionals, these children and adult children are overrepresented in nearly every casualty category—from medical, to legal, to psychological. Our challenge is to expand treatment models and utilize the unique resources and assets these populations have. We must outgrow yesterday's understandings.

This book by Pat Mansmann and Pat Neuhausel is another response to the needs of the adult children of alcoholics. Of note, this is their second edition, which attests both to their growth as well as the growth of the "adult children" movement. Addressed to therapists, their work again "hopes to lighten the load" by providing an array of tools and strategies which are interwoven through the six stages of recovery described in *Guide to Recovery: A Book for Adult Children of Alcoholics,* which has been re-published by Simon and Schuster and called *Recovery: A Guide for Adult Children of Alcoholics.*

As with my reading of their first edition, I got to see some of my thoughts reflected in ways I both intended and didn't intend. In their description of the treatment process they illustrated and interpreted many ideas expressed in *Recovery* through their own clinical experience. And that's just how it should be! While I agree with much of what they have to say, I don't agree with everything. That's just how it should be, too. Diversity as well as agreement, are necessary at this point in the growth of the movement.

It has been an honor to write this forward. Pat and Pat's book is useful, informative and full of practical, "hands on" strategies for therapists. I was often surprised by the confluence of our ideas, and I believe their book will help many practitioners with the difficult, yet rewarding, task of working with adult children of alcoholics and other trauma.

Herbert L. Gravitz, Ph.D.


For a second time I am privileged to speak to you, the reader, about this manuscript. I have recently read the additions to the original, and I am greatly pleased. Although it seems literature is abounding in the adult children's field, there has remained an obvious lack of practical treatment applications. This book takes a major step to fill that lack. Pat and Pat offer a systematic approach to treating the thousands who are now identifying as survivors of dysfunctional homes. This manuscript does not pretend to teach therapists to be therapists, but rather present tools and exercises which skilled therapists can use to enhance their work with this traumatized population.

May this small book be the pioneering work that encourages others who work in the "front trenches" to share what they have been discovering about facilitating the recovery process of adult children of alcoholics and other children of trauma. My thanks to both Pats for caring enough to take the time.

Julie D. Bowden, M.S.

# A Need for Holistic Therapy: Treating Adult Children of Alcoholics

Everyone is born into his/her family and its parentally set lifestyle by chance: however, the lifestyle one lives as an adult is by choice. Adult children of alcoholics (ACOAs) are members of families where alcoholism has existed, and denial, delusion, deception (even from self) are a part of the only lifestyle they know. The adult alcoholic usurps much of the child's role, in many cases forcing the child into a parent's role. Thus, the therapeutic approach for treating an ACOA involves the therapist and the client in the immense task of attempting to reparent the "child in the adult body."

Some element of denial is a common denominator of all behavioral problems, but the crucial difference in adult children of alcoholics is society's attitude toward the substance itself. A child growing up in an alcoholic family is bombarded with images from electronic and print media reinforcing the message that alcohol makes you happy, sexy and successful; yet at home, the same child sees alcohol as provoking rage, guilt and despair. This is a cognitive dilemma that cannot be overstated (Policoff, 1985).

Treating alcoholism and alcoholic family systems requires a special awareness from the therapist. Because dealing with the adult child involves a complete family system of several generations, the therapist cannot rely on a single method of treatment. Taking the adult child through a complete healing process, the therapist must use a multi-disciplinary approach along with a multi-generational perspective. This awareness is imperative for suc-

1

EXHIBIT 1

THERAPEUTIC LIFE CYCLE OF ADULT CHILDREN OF ALCOHOLICS

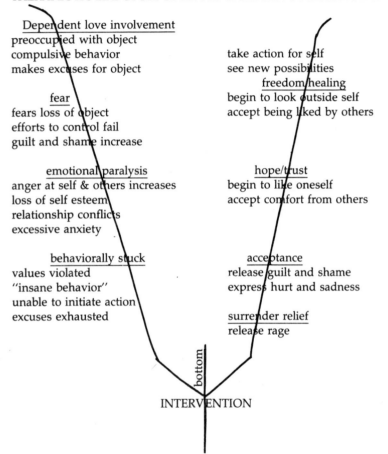

<u>Dependent love involvement</u>
preoccupied with object
compulsive behavior
makes excuses for object

<u>fear</u>
fears loss of object
efforts to control fail
guilt and shame increase

<u>emotional paralysis</u>
anger at self & others increases
loss of self esteem
relationship conflicts
excessive anxiety

<u>behaviorally stuck</u>
values violated
"insane behavior"
unable to initiate action
excuses exhausted

take action for self
see new possibilities
freedom/healing
begin to look outside self
accept being liked by others

<u>hope/trust</u>
begin to like oneself
accept comfort from others

<u>acceptance</u>
release guilt and shame
express hurt and sadness

<u>surrender relief</u>
release rage

bottom

INTERVENTION

from: <u>Choicemaking</u>, p. 23
      Sharon Wegscheider-Cruse
      Health Communications, Inc.
      1721 Blount Road, Suite 1
      Pompano Beach, FL   33069

cessful treatment. Sharon Wegscheider-Cruse, in her book *Choicemaking* (1985), indicates how complex the intervention is for the adult child. Her schematic diagram (Exhibit 1) shows the adult child's life cycle through recovery. Another model of treatment for the adult child is described by psychologist Sondra Smalley. She divides the therapy into three phases: (1) the "I" phase, in which needs and feelings are recognized and a positive inventory is formed; (2) the "me" phase, in which the client observes him/herself interacting with others and learns that s/he can be OK even when those around him/her are not; and (3) the "we" phase, in which issues of trust and control are addressed and an ability for intimacy develops (cited by Policoff, 1985). One might visualize this therapy as three interlocking circles:

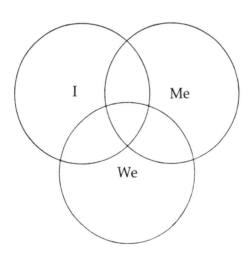

# Treatment Difficulties Specific to ACOAs

Treatment is the process of integrating what the therapist sees from the adult child and his/her family with the needed therapeutic disciplines (Treadway, 1985). The therapist must be prepared to individualize the treatment plan for the adult child. Much of the individualization will depend on the role (hero, scapegoat, lost child, mascot, etc.) the adult child played in his/her family of origin.

Adult children of alcoholics are not what they appear to be; they are both more and less than the image they project. They create an illusion that deceives both themselves and others. The presentation the client gives the therapist is in many cases one-dimensional, revealing only the strengths and masking the inadequacies, denying the paradoxical nature of his/her functioning, negating the existance of unresolved conflicts, and ignoring internal inconsistency (Balls, 1985).

Paradox, inconsistency, and unresolved conflict are certainly not unique to the ACOA, nor are they impediments to effective treatment. What is problematic is that they go unrecognized by the ACOA and possibly the therapist (Treadway, 1985).

As children, the ACOAs often appear to be responsible and mature beyond their years. They may look picture-book perfect, but many are walking time-bombs. Recent research (Black, 1982; Pickens, 1984) indicates that these children limp into adulthood with a variety of definable clinical issues (Gravitz/Bowden, 1985).

Control is a commanding need for adult children. They will go to extremes in order to be in control, and they become very apprehensive when their control is threatened. Their functioning tends to be "all-or-nothing." Both the extreme need to control and all-or-nothing functioning are at the heart of self-defeating patterns of behavior which typically characterize adult children. These behaviors are not always apparent and often are seen as positive traits since they superficially appear as extraordinary hard work and motivation. When control and all-or-nothing functioning are in full force, the anxiety, guilt and depression produced directly contribute to adult children feeling bad, sick and crazy. Thus when ACOAs are exposed to new information which is inconsistent with their self-perception, they easily become overwhelmed, confused, and frantic. Compounding the problem, ACOAs are typically unable to take things one step at a time, or break down a task into more manageable steps; so the new information intensifies their feelings of being overwhelmed and increases their desire to shut down.

When they first begin treatment, ACOAs can become so caught up in grieving or experiencing long-repressed feelings that they tell themselves:

- I'm going to get stuck here!

- I'll never get past all these emotions.

- I've got to make myself stop it.

- This isn't doing me any good; it only hurts.

- I'll cry and never stop.

- I might go crazy (Gravitz/Bowden, 1985).

As professionals we must be sensitive to the pain of recovery. Change can be very intense and also very threatening. Alcoholics Anonymous (AA) lessons such as "one day at a time" and "easy does it" are pertinent to adult children also.

The therapist must be steeped in the AA philosophy and principles in order to work with ACOAs. In fact, a therapist who is not aware of and does not practice the AA and Al-Anon principles such as enabling and detachment can bring more harm than help to the client.

Likewise, a therapist who has not been aware of and dealt with his/her own ACOA issues can also do the client a great disservice. Research suggests that as many as 80% of all helping professionals are ACOAs, and therapists can not help their clients heal if they are not in the healing process themselves. We realize that none of us is void of issues, but therapists need to be aware of unresolved issues of their own that may interfere with the therapy of the client. Issues that particularly complicate therapy if the therapist is not able to deal with them are: denial (even the therapist's own denial), enabling, detachment, control, confronting and self caring. As one can surmise, doing ACOA therapy requires the therapist to be a healthy, growing adult.

In order for treatment to be successful, it is very important for the therapist to be able to deal with all of the above issues. ACOA therapy emphasizes these issues of denial, detachment, etc., much more than many of the other psychodynamic therapies. Enabling is one aspect of the therapy that many times plays a pivotal role in successful treatment. It is important for the therapist to remember that if s/he enables the client, the disease is continued and progresses in severity.

Enabling in many cases is not what is appears to be to the outside world. It could "look like" being helpful to the client, but in reality the action does much harm. Doing enabling behavior can create a "rescuing therapist which would recreate a duplication of the pathogenic family system" (Friesen and Casella, 1982). A few examples of therapists repeating the dysfunction through enabling behavior are the following:

- denying alcoholism and the alcoholic family system (by not taking a complete history or giving assessments).

- doing for the client what the client can do for him/herself.

- allowing the client to continue in therapy while not following any program.

- believing that s/he (the therapist) can supply to the client what the client did not get in the family of origin (not teaching self-caring behavior; making client dependent on the therapist).

- denying needed support and encouragement to clients for actual separation from family members when such separation is needed for client's recovery.

Another aspect of the ACOA therapy that presents treatment difficulties to the therapist is that the primary problem (although rarely the presenting problem) is that of being an ACOA—needing to develop adult skills and re-parent the "child within" in a safe environment. Many of the symptoms that the ACOA presents to the therapist mimic several of the mental health disorders—depression, anxiety, cocaine addiction, etc. The therapists must not be sidetracked or do "bandaid on cancer" therapy by focusing only on the anxiety, depression, relationship problems, etc. These are the results of the ACOA's lack of adult emotional skills. Unless the client develops these basic skills whose development was thwarted in childhood, the best that can be expected from therapy is temporary relief. ACOA therapy is directed towards permanent change through skill building for that child in the adult body. The therapist needs to realize that depression, anxiety, etc., result from a child's living and surviving in a dysfunctional family, and are normal and appropriate feelings for such a life. Once the adult child leaves that setting, many of these skills, which were functional in his/her dysfunctional family, cease to serve their once-helpful purpose—and may in fact serve to continue the dysfunctional cycle. Yet they are deeply ingrained, so that they do not disappear miraculously when they are no longer needed.

The therapist must help the adult child recognize that these dysfunctional "survival skills" once were valuable but now can stand in the way of his/her creating a healthier life for him/herself. It is the therapist along with the therapeutic environment, who provides courage and safety for the adult child to change those skills and to grow into a functional adult. One possible course is to help the adult child incorporate his/her survival skills (which in many cases are in the extreme range) with adult skills. When s/he succeeds in this aim, the therapist sees the presenting problem (anxiety, depression, etc.) becoming less apparent and less significant.

# Stages of Treatment

A sequential recovery continuum is consistent with what AA has successfully known and followed for years. Recovery needs to be a series of stages, and it is important to proceed through these stages sequentially. However, in therapy, it is found that clients may be at the end of one stage, feeling "cured," but only just beginning another stage. Since adult children have in many cases lived chaotic and confused lives, the order produced by a recovery continuum is a significant change in itself (Gravitz/Bowden, 1985). Order and sequence are important for ACOAs because chaos is the norm in the alcoholic family. Without this sequential order in recovery, the ACOA will relive the chaos in therapy and bounce from stage to stage without completing anything. These stages of recovery are described by Gravitz and Bowden:

First stage — Survival

Second stage — Emergent Awareness

Third stage — Core Issues

Fourth stage — Transformations

Fifth stage — Integration

Sixth stage — Genesis

Stages of Recovery

# First Stage—Survival

"The first stage of recovery is the survival of childhood." (Gravitz/Bowden, 1985). Reared by parents who too often could not provide for their needs, these adult children made it through childhood, but at a cost. Their emotional development is in many cases frozen at an early age, and they may be burned out upon entering early adulthood. In varying degrees of emotional and physical pain, ACOAs typically make few connections between their current problems as adults and the familial alcoholism. They are prone to psychosomatic illnesses, eating disorders, depression, and a host of other problems (McKenna, 1981). Only an intervention and breaking the cycle can save them from repeating generational problems of chemical dependency or other addictive behaviors.

Very often adult children are in the survival stage when they come to therapy. The important consequence of this stage is how the childhood experiences are affecting their present adult life. Many times the client comes into treatment because of adult problems—divorce, physical illness, child-rearing difficulties, etc.—and the therapist discovers that familial alcoholism is the underlying cause.

Like alcoholism, the problems that beset ACOAs are based in tremendous denial and a therapist's first task is to properly identify these clients. Before working on the ACOA issues, one must be sure that the client is neither an alcoholic nor a drug user at present, and, if there is a history of addiction, that s/he is well into recovery (Sharon Wegscheider-Cruse indicates that the ACOA should be at least one year into recovery.)

Three assessment tools that can be used to identify the alcoholic or adult child on a progression scale are found in Exhibits 2, 3 and 4. In administering the MAST to a client, in many cases we find that s/he is also alcoholic. If the client is resistant to this notion, we use two other tools to help him/her own the alcoholism—the Johns Hopkins twenty questions, and reporting from family members if that is available. The Friel Co-Dependency and CAST assessments allow the client to own behaviors and experiences that have happened/or are continually happening in his/her life. Both also provide information to the client as to how severe the disease is and how it has affected him/her. An additional assessment tool that McKenna & Pickens (McKenna, 1983) have found to indicate significant scores of personality traits of the alcoholic is the Minnesota Multiphasic Personality Inventory (MMPI).

EXHIBIT 2

MICHIGAN ALCOHOL SCREENING TEST—MAST

Questionnaire About Drinking Habits

| | Yes | No |
|---|---|---|
| Do you enjoy a drink now and then? | 0 | |
| Do you feel you are a normal drinker? | | 2 |
| (By normal we mean you drink less than or as much as most other people). | | |
| Have you ever awakened the morning after some drinking the night before and found that you could not remember a part of the evening? | 2 | |
| Does your wife, husband, a parent, or other near relative, ever worry or complain about your drinking? | 2 | |
| Can you stop drinking without a struggle after one or two drinks? | | 2 |
| Do you feel guilty about your drinking? | 1 | |
| Do friends or relatives think you are a normal drinker? | | 2 |
| Are you able to stop drinking when you want to? | | 2 |
| Have you ever attended a meeting of Alcoholics Anonymous (AA)? | 5 | |
| Have you gotten into physical fights when drinking? | 1 | |
| Has your drinking ever created problems between you and your wife, husband, a parent or another relative? | 2 | |
| Has your wife, husband (or other family members) ever gone to anyone for help about your drinking? | 2 | |
| Have you ever lost friends because of your drinking? | 2 | |
| Have you ever gotten into trouble at school or work because of drinking? | 2 | |
| Have you ever lost a job because of drinking? | 2 | |
| Have you ever neglected your obligations, your family, or your work for two or more days in a row because you were drinking? | 2 | |

EXHIBIT 2 Continued

| | | |
|---|---|---|
| Do you drink before noon fairly often? | 1 | ___ |
| Have you ever been told you have liver trouble? Cirrhosis? | 2 | ___ |
| After heavy drinking have you ever had Delirium Tremens (D.T.'s) or severe shaking, or heard voices or seen things that really weren't there? | 2* | ___ |
| Have you ever gone to anyone for help about your drinking? | 2 | ___ |
| Have you ever been in a hospital because of drinking? | 5 | ___ |
| Have you ever been a patient in a psychiatric hospital or on a psychiatric ward of a general hospital where drinking was part of the problem that resulted in hospitalization? | 5 | ___ |
| Have you ever been seen at a psychiatric or mental health clinic or gone to any doctor, social worker, or clergyman for help with any emotional problem, where drinking was part of the problem? | 2 | ___ |
| Have you ever been arrested for drunk driving, driving while intoxicated, or driving under the influence of alcoholic beverages? | 2† | ___ |
| Have you ever been arrested, or taken into custody, even for a few hours, because of other drunken behavior? (IF YES, How many times?) | 2† | ___ |

*5 points for Delirium Tremens
†2 points for each arrest.

SCORING SYSTEM: In general, five points or more would place the subject in an "alcoholic" category. Four points would be suggestive of alcoholism, three points or less would indicate the subject was not alcoholic.

Programs using the above scoring system find it very sensitive at the five-point level, and it tends to find more people alcoholic than anticipated. However, because it is a screening test, it should be this sensitive at its lower levels.

Most alcoholics score 10 points or more.

EXHIBIT 3

CO-DEPENDENCY ASSESSMENT INVENTORY

by John C. Friel, Ph.D

FCA DEMOGRAPHIC SURVEY

Age _____Sex _____Occupation _____

Race: Caucasian    Black    Mexican-American    Native American
    Oriental    Other _____
Marital Status: Married    Single    Divorced    Widowed    Remarried
Educational Level: 1st–8th    9th    10th    11th    12th    College 1    College 2
    College 3    College 4    Master's Degree    Ph.D., M.D., LL.D.
    Other _____
Spouse's Age _____ Spouse's Occupation _____
Number of Children: 1    2    3    4    5    6    7    Other _____
Yearly    Gross    Family    Income:    0–$11,999    $12,000–$19,999
    $20,000–$29,999    $30,000–39,999    $40,000–49,999    $50,000 or more
Have you ever had problems with chemical dependency or abuse?
    yes    no
Has anyone in your immediate family ever had problems with chemical
    dependency or abuse? (father, mother, brother, sister)    yes    no
Has anyone in your extended family ever had problems with chemical
    dependency or abuse? (aunt, uncle, cousin, grandparent)    yes    no
During the past year, have you had any of the following stress-related
    problems or symptoms? (high blood pressure, tension headache, mi-
    graine headache, ulcer, asthma, muscle tension, teeth grinding, sore
    jaw joints, etc.)    yes    no
How about anyone in your immediate family?    yes    no
In your extended family?    yes    no
Anyone close to you, but not in your family?    yes    no
How satisfied are you with your work and career life?    1 2 3 4 5 6 7
                Not at all        Very much
How satisfied are you with the number and quality of your friendships?
    1 2 3 4 5 6 7
How satisfied are you with your relationship with your mate, partner,
    or spouse?    1 2 3 4 5 6 7
Below are a number of questions dealing with how you feel about
yourself, your life, and those around you. As you answer each question,
be sure to answer honestly, but do not spend too much time dwelling

EXHIBIT 3 Continued

on any one question. There are no right or wrong answers. Take each question as it comes and answer as you usually feel.

T  F  1. I make enough time to do things just for myself each week.

T  F  2. I spend lots of time criticizing myself after an interaction with someone.

T  F  3. I would not be embarrassed if people knew certain things about me.

T  F  4. Sometimes I feel like I just waste a lot of time and don't get anywhere.

T  F  5. I take good enough care of myself.

T  F  6. It is usually best not to tell someone they bother you; it only causes fights and gets everyone upset.

T  F  7. I am happy about the way my family communicated when I was growing up.

T  F  8. Sometimes I don't know how I really feel.

T  F  9. I am very satisfied with my intimate love life.

T  F  10. I've been feeling tired lately.

T  F  11. When I was growing up, my family liked to talk openly about problems.

T  F  12. I often look happy when I am sad or angry.

T  F  13. I am satisfied with the number and kind of relationships I have in my life.

T  F  14. Even if I had the time and money to do it, I would feel uncomfortable taking a vacation by myself.

T  F  15. I have enough help with everything I must do each day.

T  F  16. I wish that I could accomplish a lot more than I do now.

T  F  17. My family taught me to express feelings and affection openly when I was growing up.

T  F  18. It is hard for me to talk to someone in authority. (boss, teachers, etc.)

T  F  19. When I am in a relationship that becomes too confusing and complicated, I have no trouble getting out of it.

T  F  20. I sometimes feel pretty confused about who I am and where I want to go with my life.

T  F  21. I am satisfied with the way that I take care of my own needs.

T  F  22. I am not satisfied with my career.

T  F  23. I usually handle my problems calmly and directly.

EXHIBIT 3 Continued

T  F  24. I hold back my feelings much of the time because I don't want to hurt other people or have them think less of me.

T  F  25. I don't feel like I'm "in a rut" very often.

T  F  26. I am not satisfied with my friendships.

T  F  27. When someone hurts my feelings or does something that I don't like I have little difficulty telling them about it.

T  F  28. When a close friend or relative asks for my help more than I'd like, I usually say "yes" anyway.

T  F  29. I love to face new problems and am good at finding solutions to them.

T  F  30. I do not feel good about my childhood.

T  F  31. I am not concerned about my health a lot.

T  F  32. I often feel like no one really knows me.

T  F  33. I feel calm and peaceful most of the time.

T  F  34. I find it difficult to ask for what I want.

T  F  35. I don't let people take advantage of me more than I'd like.

T  F  36. I am dissatisfied with at least one of my close relationships.

T  F  37. I make major decisions quite easily.

T  F  38. I don't trust myself in new situations as much as I'd like.

T  F  39. I am very good at knowing when to speak up and when to go along with others' wishes.

T  F  40. I wish I had more time away from my work.

T  F  41. I am as spontaneous as I'd like to be.

T  F  42. Being alone is a problem for me.

T  F  43. When someone I love is bothering me, I have no problem telling them so.

T  F  44. I often have so many things going on at once that I'm really not doing justice to any one of them.

T  F  45. I am very comfortable letting others into my life and revealing "the real me" to them.

T  F  46. I apologize to others too much for what I do or say.

T  F  47. I have no problem telling people when I am angry with them.

T  F  48. There's so much to do and not enough time. Sometimes I'd like to leave it all behind me.

T  F  49. I have few regrets about what I have done with my life.

T  F  50. I tend to think of others more than I do of myself.

EXHIBIT 3 Continued

T  F  51. More often than not, my life has gone the way that I wanted it to.
T  F  52. People admire me because I'm so understanding of others, even when they do something that annoys me.
T  F  53. I am comfortable with my own sexuality.
T  F  54. I sometimes feel embarrassed by behaviors of those close to me.
T  F  55. The important people in my life know "the real me," and I am okay with them knowing.
T  F  56. I do my share of work, and often do quite a bit more.
T  F  57. I do not feel that everything would fall apart without my efforts and attention.
T  F  58. I do too much for other people and then later wonder why I did so.
T  F  59. I am happy about the way my family coped with problems when I was growing up.
T  F  60. I wish that I had more people to do things with.

Scoring

All odd-numbered answers must be reflected, i.e., reversed, before summing up for a total score. Thus, if the answer is "T" to item #1, it should be reversed to "F" before adding up the total. This is because half the items are worded in the co-dependent direction while half are not, to control for acquiescent response sets. The total score is then the sum of all "T" answers after reflection.

We have found scores below 20 to indicate few co-dependent concerns; 21-30 to be mild/moderate; 31–45 moderate/severe; and over 45; severe.

(An answer sheet can be typed with five columns, numbers 1–12, 13–24, etc. which makes reflection of odd-numbered items much simpler. With this arrangement, all items in odd-numbered rows are reflected.)

EXHIBIT 4

CHILDREN OF ALCOHOLIC SCREENING TEST—C.A.S.T.

C.A.S.T. can be used to identify latency-age, adolescent, and grown-up children of alcoholics.

Please check () the answer below that best describes your feelings, behavior, and experiences related to a parent's alcohol use. Take your time and be as accurate as possible. Answer all 30 questions by checking either "yes" or "no."

Yes  No

1. Have you ever thought that one of your parents had a drinking problem?

2. Have you ever lost sleep because of a parent's drinking?

3. Did you ever encourage one of your parents to quit drinking?

4. Did you ever feel alone, scared, nervous, angry or frustrated because a parent was not able to stop drinking?

5. Did you ever argue or fight with a parent when he or she was drinking?

6. Did you ever threaten to run away from home because of a parent drinking?

7. Has a parent ever yelled at or hit you or other family members when drinking?

8. Have you ever heard your parents fight when one of them was drunk?

9. Did you ever protect another family member from a parent who was drinking?

10. Did you ever feel like hiding or emptying a parent's bottle of liquor?

11. Do many of your thoughts revolve around a problem-drinking parent or difficulties that arise because of his or her drinking?

12. Did you ever wish that a parent would stop drinking?

13. Did you ever feel responsible for and guilty about a parent's drinking?

14. Did you ever fear that your parents would get divorced due to alcohol misuse?

EXHIBIT 4 Continued

\_\_\_ \_\_\_ 15. Have you ever withdrawn from and avoided outside activities and friends because of embarrassment and shame over a parent's drinking problem?

\_\_\_ \_\_\_ 16. Did you ever feel caught in the middle of an argument or fight between a problem-drinking parent and your other parent?

\_\_\_ \_\_\_ 17. Did you ever feel that you made a parent drink alcohol?

\_\_\_ \_\_\_ 18. Have you ever felt that a problem—drinking parent did not really love you?

\_\_\_ \_\_\_ 19. Did you ever resent a parent's drinking?

\_\_\_ \_\_\_ 20. Have you ever worried about a parent's health because of his or her alcohol use?

\_\_\_ \_\_\_ 21. Have you ever been blamed for a parent's drinking?

\_\_\_ \_\_\_ 22. Did you ever think your father was an alcoholic?

\_\_\_ \_\_\_ 23. Did you ever wish your home could be more like the homes of your friends who did not have a parent with a drinking problem?

\_\_\_ \_\_\_ 24. Did a parent ever make promises to you that he or she did not keep because of drinking?

\_\_\_ \_\_\_ 25. Did you ever think your mother was an alcoholic?

\_\_\_ \_\_\_ 26. Did you ever wish that you could talk to some one who could understand and help the alcohol-related problems in your family?

\_\_\_ \_\_\_ 27. Did you ever fight with your brothers and sisters about a parent's drinking?

\_\_\_ \_\_\_ 28. Did you ever stay away from home to avoid the drinking parent or your other parent's reaction to the drinking?

\_\_\_ \_\_\_ 29. Have you ever felt sick, cried, or had a "knot" in your stomach after worrying about a parent's drinking?

\_\_\_ \_\_\_ 30. Did you ever take over any chores and duties at home that were usually done by a parent before he or she developed a drinking problem?

\_\_\_TOTAL NUMBER OF 'YES' ANSWERS.

Score of 6 or more means that more than likely this child is the child of an alcoholic parent.

© 1982 by John W. Jones, Ph.D, Family Recovery Press.

It is also very important for the therapist to take a thorough individual and family history. By using all of the assessment tools and being aware of the strength of denial in these families, the therapist may prevent him/herself from missing the major problem (alcoholism) in the family's life. Some studies indicate that as many as 50% of excessive drinkers go undiagnosed (Howland, 1985). Because of the positive external presentation of an adult child, an even greater percentage of ACOAs could go undiagnosed.

Another important tool in the assessment of the adult child is the genogram. It indicates the three-generational transmittal of particular alcoholic patterns and influences. Many times the adult child is not aware of (or won't admit) who in her/his family are/were alcoholics. This skeletal genogram can be very helpful in showing the influence of alcoholism in the family. Later, the therapist can embellish the genogram to indicate more elaborate behavioral patterns between family members so that the adult child can better understand the effect of the disease.

In addition to the above assessments, Arnold Lazarus' Multimodal Life History Questionnaire is also very valuable. This gives the therapist an overall view of the client's general information, description of presenting problems, personal and social history, behavior, feelings, physical sensations, images, thoughts, interpersonal relationships, and biological factors. It is a long assessment and takes some time and emotional energy to complete. Clients report many positive results from doing this assessment—becoming consciously aware of and admitting parts of their lives, allowing themselves to be honest and expose/explore parts of their lives they have not examined before, seeing patterns in their lives, etc.

A client may come to therapy at any of a number of awareness levels, from having no knowledge about adult children of alcoholics to having been in therapy for quite a long time and/or having "researched" or read on the topic quite extensively. It is the therapist's job to determine where the awareness of the client lies on the spectrum and what will best suit his/her needs, using assessment instruments, closely monitoring treatment, and providing a variety of experiences.

In helping the client gain maximum benefit from the entire ACOA treatment, a therapeutic rule of no drinking or drugs is given for the duration of treatment. The client is generally growing much faster than a normal life pattern (going emotionally from a 2- to 5-year-old to an adult), and the surge of emotions s/he experiences, perhaps for the first time ever, may feel like a flood—or a roller coaster. During all these times, it is very important that the client is totally present to all that is happening and not be altered by any drug. This therapeutic rule also allows the therapist to monitor the treatment better, and to know if drugs are a problem.

# Second Stage—Emergent Awareness

"Once aware of their genetic, physiological, sociological, and psychological vulnerabilities, adult children enter the second stage of recovery, emergent awareness." They recognize that something was wrong in childhood, and they no longer need to deny it to be safe. Acknowledgement of past experiences becomes the key to unlocking the self-validation essential to understanding and coping with present-day life. The self-identification as the child of an alcoholic creates a whirlpool of feelings that push them toward taking significant therapeutic steps for themselves. Several of these tasks include: mourning a lost childhood, learning to accept their experiences as legitimate, learning to listen to their inner voice, learning to be gentle with themselves, and learning to ask for help (Gravitz/Bowden, 1985).

To help a client process these tasks, the therapist can use various therapeutic tools (which can be employed throughout all six stages of recovery). One such tool is journal writing, which helps the client to make sense out of chaos, identify "stuffed" feelings, write down thoughts before acting compulsively, reflect feelings on various levels, and build a plan of action.

Journal writing is probably one of the most vaulable tools in ACOA therapy. Clients are assigned journal writing as early as their first or second session. Many clients have done different kinds of journal writing before, but we encourage them to focus on feelings as opposed to reporting their day's activities. A client might, for example, begin journal writing by writing three feelings a day. To help the client become more aware of feelings, we give lists of feeling words and pictures of faces expressing feelings. We take much time discussing feelings with the client, hoping that may give him/her permission to feel. One important point we discuss is the difference between feelings and thoughts. In the beginning of identification of feelings, the client usually reports feelings of sadness, anger, and loneliness.

Journal entries need to be dated for several reasons:

- to help therapist and client to be aware of troublesome patterns of behavior.

- to track patterns of emotions or behaviors.

- to monitor these patterns.

Often the client will begin journal writing with a free-flowing style, just recording thoughts and feelings as they come to mind. Later, we suggest a more sophisticated writing (called refuting journal writing) using the following structure: the client begins by identfying a feeling or thought. If s/he first identifies a feeling, s/he then puts down the thought connected with the feeling. If s/he has identified a thought, s/he then puts down the feeling connected with the thought. Next, if these thoughts are irrational, the client can refute them. In the refuting process, the client lists statements showing that the original thought does not make sense and that he/she can think in a healthier way. This enables the client to take charge of the feeling also. The next phase of the journal entry is to focus on the feelings, thoughts, and refuted thoughts, and to come up with a plan (what will I do about this?). The plan must be:

- within the capability range of the client.

- specific.

- sequential.

The client must make a commitment to follow the plan to completion. ACOAs tend to overgeneralize and not complete tasks, so s/he needs to make sure the plan is "chunked-down" in order not to be overwhelmed by it.

The client should read over the plan many times in order to remind him/her of the commitment and to increase therapeutic benefit. The following artwork on the next three pages is a plan developed by a client in order to make a phone call to his brother.

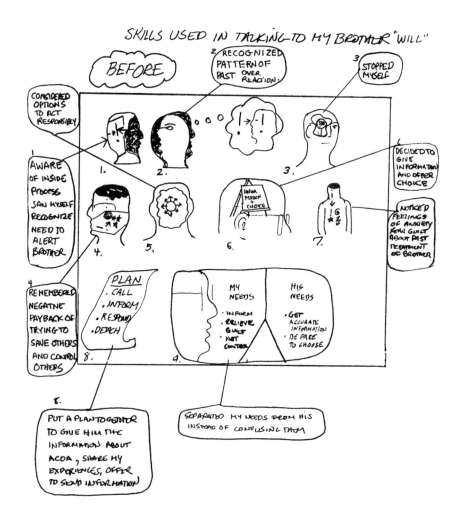

SKILLS USED IN TALKING TO MY BROTHER "WILL"

The final phase of the refuting journal writing is "completing the cycle." After s/he has carried out the plan, the client "completes the cycle" of this new behavior by stroking and affirming him/herself for the success. This is a very important part of the behavior change. It allows the client to take charge of incorporating his/her own thoughts and feelings rather than living by dysfunctional thoughts and feelings from his/her family of origin. The stroking also provides a reinforcement for this new pattern of behavior, increasing the likelihood that the client will use his/her new pattern of refuting the next time a similar dysfunctional feeling or thought is present.

Overall, journal writing is, for many, the key that keeps the therapy on track. Clients may be resistant to journal writing in the beginning, because they may be experiencing too many emotions (so they think) and feel out of control. One client who was very resistant to journal writing in her initial stages of therapy became very dedicated to it as she found that it was through journal writing that she became herself. She wrote a letter to describe to other clients the importance journal writing had for her.

Dear Friends:
    I want to share the importance of journal writing for me. During my therapy, when it was suggested that I write daily about my feelings, I had all kinds of excuses. My biggest excuse was I felt it was a waste of time when I could just sit quietly and think about what I was feeling. That was my biggest mistake. When I would attempt to deal with feelings that way, several things would happen. I would try to control the feelings, make a catastrophe out of the thought or feeling, or I would fantasize. I got into a lot of all-or-nothing thinking. All of the above only produced more anxiety. By writing I was able to stay more in reality.
    I usually write in the morning, since I awaken early and lie

thinking before starting my day. Most of the time my writing starts with a thought which will trigger a feeling or many feelings. I will then search for the reasons for my feelings and then write them down. In my case these are usually some kind of fear. Then I will ask myself if that fear really fits in my world today as an adult or is it a carryover from childhood. My last steps are to make a decision as to what I am going to do about it and how I can best accomplish that goal. After this process, everything becomes much clearer and I can usually let go of my faulty thinking. Sometimes I may have to write the same thing several times before I can come to a resolution.

Because I was so resistant to writing, I was relapsing frequently. After being told constantly to write each time this would happen, I finally took on the responsibility of doing this for myself daily. By doing this I have been better able to stay in reality. My biggest problem in the beginning was I was unable to identify a feeling. My therapist gave me a great list of feelings, and by identifying three feelings a day and each week increasing the number, I finally began to recognize what I was feeling. After I was able to identify the feelings, the journal writing became an invaluable tool for me. I had gotten a lot of awareness in private therapy and had developed several skills; but journal writing is very important because it helps to keep me in the present by practicing what I learned in therapy.

Another tip which I found helpful is to treat yourself to a nice writing book or pad that is pretty and cheerful. It gives me more inspiration to write than does just thinking about opening a drab spiral notebook. Remember you are worth whatever it takes to get and keep you writing.

I will close wishing you much success and serenity. Keep writing!!

Love,
Felicia

Another important therapeutic tool is bibliotherapy. Reading about alcoholism in general and specifically about the adult child syndrome helps the adult child gain a clearer understanding of self and family. Readings also give the client a variety of resources that can be helpful to move him/her forward or to provide more accurate information. A partial list of books for bibliotherapy use is found in Exhibit 5. The therapist must identify the relevant issues, in the readings, e.g., money, procrastination, workaholism, sex, intimacy, etc.—to the individual client to make the reading pertinent.

EXHIBIT 5

READINGS FOR BIBLIOTHERAPY

Bach, Richard. *The Bridge Across Forever*. New York: William Morrow & Company, Inc., 1984.

Barbach, Lonnie Garfield, Ph.D. *For Yourself: The Fulfillment of Female Sexuality*. New York: Signet, 1975.

Burka, Jane B., Ph.D. and Lenora M. Yuen, Ph.D. *Procrastination*. Reading: Addison-Wesley Publishing Company, 1983.

Buscaglia, Leo, Ph.D. *Living, Loving & Learning*. Thorofare: Charles B. Slack, Inc., 1982.

Carson, Richard Davis. *Taming Your Gremlin*. Dallas: The Family Resource, Inc., 1983.

Colgrove, Melba, Ph.D. et al. *How to Survive the Loss of a Love*. New York: Bantam Books, 1976.

Friedman, Meyer, M.D. and Diane Ulmer, R.N., M.S. *Treating Type A Behavior & Your Heart*. New York: Alfred A. Knopf, 1984.

Friends in Recovery. *The Twelves Steps—A Way Out*. San Diego: Recovery Publications, 1987.

Goldberg, Herb, Ph.D. and Robert T. Lewis, Ph.D. *Money Madness*. New York: The New American Library, Inc., 1978.

Halpern, Howard M., Ph.D. *How to Break Your Addiction to a Person*. New York: Bantam Books, 1982.

Herrigel, Eugene. *Zen and the Art of Archery*. New York: Vintage Books, 1971.

Hollis, Judi, Ph.D. *Fat Is a Family Affair*. Minneapolis: Hazeldon Educational Materials, 1985.

Hutchinson, Marcia Germaine, Ed.D. *Transforming Body Image*. Trumansburg: The Crossing Press, 1985.

James, Muriel. *It's Never Too Late To Be Happy*. Reading: Addison-Wesley Publishing Company, Inc., 1985.

Kennedy, Eugene. *Loneliness & Everyday Problems*. Garden City: Image Books, 1983.

Krimmel, Edward & Patricia. *The Low Blood Sugar Handbook*. Bryn Mawr: Franklin Publishers, 1984.

Larson, Earnie. *Stage II Relationships–Love Beyond Addiction*. San Francisco: Harper & Row Publishers, 1987.

Lerner, Rokelle. *Daily Affirmations*. Pompano Beach: Health Communications, Inc., 1985.

Lindquist, Marie. *Holding Back*. Minneapolis: Hazeldon Educational Materials, 1987.

Milam, James R. & Katherine Ketcham. *Under the Influence*. Seattle: Madrona Publishers, 1981.

Nerin, William S. *Family Reconstruction*. New York: W.W. Norton & Company, 1986.

Norwood, Robin. *Women Who Love Too Much*. Los Angeles: Jeremy P. Tarcher, Inc., 1985.

Peck, Scott M., M.D. *The Road Less Traveled*. New York: Simon & Schuster, 1978.

Peele, Stanton with Archie Brodsky. *Love Addiction*. New York: New American Library, 1975.

Powell, John, S.J. *The Secret of Staying in Love*. Allen: Argus Communications, 1974.

Powell, John, S. J. *Will the Real Me Please Stand Up?* Allen: Argus Communications, 1985.

Satir, Virginia. *Making Contact*. Berkeley: Celestial Arts, 1976.

Silverstein, Shel. *The Missing Piece Meets the Big O*. New York: Harper & Row Publishers, Inc., 1981.

Smith, Manual J., Ph.D. *When I Say No I Feel Guilty*. New York: Bantam Books, 1975.

Viscott, David, M.D. *Risking*. New York: Simon & Schuster, Inc., 1977.

Wegscheider-Cruse, Sharon. *Learning To Love Yourself*. Pompano Beach: Health Communications, 1987.

Wholey, Dennis. *The Courage To Change*. Boston: Warner Books Edition, 1984.

Zilbergeld, Bernie, Ph.D. *Male Sexuality*. New York: Bantam Books, 1978.

Support groups are a very important adjunct to the entire therapeutic process and lifetime of the adult child. Certainly if the client is an alcoholic, AA is a must. If the adult child is non-alcoholic, Al-Anon and ACOA groups are very important to the process. It is in these support groups that experiences, feelings and behaviors are shared by those with a common history. Support groups also provide a new type of environment for the participants. At these meetings clients can associate with people whose goals are similar to their own. Perhaps the most important of these goals is establishing healthy relationships with a variety of individuals.

Since there is a high rate of recovery for people using AA, it seems important to use this or another support group as an adjunct to therapy. It is not always easy to encourage the client in early recovery, who may be frightened and in pain, to trust the therapist, much less a group in the community where neighbors and fellow employees may see them. The therapist must be very firm at this point because if the client sees a way out of going to meetings, s/he may take it. Being firm may even require the therapist to take the "tough love" stand, stating "I don't accept clients unless they agree to attend appropriate support-group meetings." In our practice, we take the route of providing support to the reluctant client, increasing his/her awareness by recommending readings and identifying a contact person in the group whom the client can take to and meet at the first meeting. Often we recommended the books *Under the Influence* or *The Courage To Change* as awareness reading for alcoholic clients who show reluctance to attend meetings.

Once the client is comfortable at meetings, we encourage him/her to take an active part in the meetings—sharing, participate in activities, sharing his/her story, chairing meetings, etc. The writing below is a sharing of a client at an ACOA meeting about his awareness of his child within and the development of the relationship.

### Hi Everyone, My Name Is Jim

Not too long ago Jane asked me if I would speak at one of the meetings she chaired. She asked me if I would speak to you about my child within and the relationship I'm developing with him. I told her that I'd like to give it a shot, and here I am. My child is basically "me as a little boy." He's the part of me that I never allowed to grow up because of my disease of co-dependency. I call him Jimmy, and he calls me Daddy, because I need to do the job of parenting him that my alcoholic father couldn't. The first time I contacted him I just did it because I was told to. I was a little skeptical, but I contacted him anyway, concerning my fear of rejection. When I did, it was like I was an adult looking down on this little boy who was sitting on a bench crying; he thought his Little League coach didn't like him, because he didn't play as much as some of the other boys. It didn't occur to him that the other boys were better players. He could only see the rejection and lack of approval, just like from his daddy. That's when I introduced myself to him. I told him that I approve of him, and I love him, and that I'll always be there for him. I guess I've told him that a hundred times by now, and I'll probably need to tell him 200 more times before he's convinced and completely trusts me.

When I first met Jimmy, I called him Luke Skywalker, because I compared the program to Star Wars. I kept hearing Obi-wan Kenobi saying "Use the force, Luke" and thinking about my higher power; and Darth Vader saying "Search your feelings, Luke," and thinking about allowing myself to feel the pain and fear that have been bottled up inside me all these years.

My child is the key to all of the issues. He's afraid to fail. He's afraid of rejection. He's afraid of being abandoned and left all alone. And when I'm teaching him that he's special and telling him that I love him and will always be there for him, it takes away just a little bit of his fear, and in focusing on me and on what I'm telling him, he's not trying to control anybody or anything.

As adult children, we are very good at telling others what they should do or shouldn't do, so I use this concept by separating the healthy adult in me from the child. This simplifies the interaction with Jimmy.

It sounds very easy, but it's not. Nothing worthwhile usually is. Showing tough love to yourself is very hard to do. I'll give you an example; I have a love addiction, and the object of my addiction is the person I'm married to. I've been working hard to break this addiction and part of that was to stop clinging to her. She was my child's security blanket. So I told my child that he needed to cling to me, because I'm the only one who's always going to be here for him. Well, I would wake up in the middle of the night and I would sense this presence reaching out to touch my wife, and I would grab the hand to stop it. Boy was I surprised to find that hand attached to my arm; so I had to scold Jimmy and tell him that if he didn't stop doing that, I wouldn't let him touch her at all. To this day he needs to depend on me, and I'm looking forward to the day when Jimmy & I can stand on our own two feet.

Love,
Jim

ACOA therapy is long and arduous, requiring a strong commitment and much reinforcement to help the client understand recovery concepts. Therapy can take from two to five years, and the therapist should be aware of the expense that the client must endure. In order to stretch the client's therapy dollars, the therapist can suggest they attend workshops in the community to reinforce their therapy. For this reason, therapists need to investigate the availability of services which are usually low in cost, provided by outside community agencies such as school district night schools or YMCAs.

Attending workshops at outside agencies provides practice in assertiveness and independence, and helps the client not to become overly dependent on the primary therapist. Another benefit is that clients are able to be networked into a wider circle of positive-thinking people at a critical time when they need to detach from unhealthy relationships. Using these resources may help the client to cut down the time needed in therapy as well as expense.

Another one of the ways that we use to have the therapy extend itself from session to session is by using "GOs" (growth opportunitites). "GOs" are basically homework assignments, but we use the concept of allowing the client to choose to develop more growth (taking on the adult posture), rather than telling the client to do something if s/he knows what is good for her/him (taking on the all too familiar posture of the parent-child). By being conscientious about doing the "GOs," the client generally feels more positive about the growth process and the therapy moves forward more fully. A client's resisting doing a "GO" can make the therapist aware that an issue may be difficult for him/her (and therefore may need more processing or more time). A client's continually resisting doing a "GO" may indicate that s/he is not ready for or not committed to the therapeutic process.

In order to structure an appropriate "GO" as a result of a particular session, the therapist needs to consider several things:

• the theme of the session just completed.

• the general direction of the therapy at the time.

• the readiness and development of the client.

• the needs of the client.

"GOs" may be written work in the journal, self-caring or play activities, interactions with other people, or anything that helps the client move forward to become a more nurturing, healthy adult. Some examples of "GOs" are as follows:

Theme: Affirmations

"GO." Write two affirmations per day and repeat them often during the day. (We introduce Rokelle Lerner's *Daily Affirmations* at this time and encourage all clients to read daily from it or other appropriate affirmation books.) A client's pictorial affirmation is below.

Theme: Identify Feelings

"GO": From the feeling list, identify two feelings a day and write about the situation around the feelings. Also identify what the bodily sensations were with the feelings.

Theme: Unable to Relax

"GO": Take 5 minutes a day by yourself in a quiet, safe area to sit and relax, focusing only on breathing. Write about how it feels to give yourself permission to do this.

Theme: No Play

"GO": Three times a week, spend an hour doing a playful activity of your choice.

Theme: Separation—Detachment

"GO": Write a goodbye letter to whomever you are in an unhealthy relationship with (father, mother, spouse, etc.).

Below are several examples of clients' detachment letters.

## PHIL'S LETTER TO FATHER

Dear Daddy,

I have a bone to pick with you; actually several bones. I know that you're dead and could care less about what I'm going to tell you, but I'm gonna tell you anyway.

I didn't ask to be born. If you and Mama made a mistake and conceived me, that was your fault, not mine. I didn't asked to be born intelligent, but you rejected me for having a gift that you and Mama gave me.

You punished me when I told you a lie, but when I was honest and pointed out your "mistake" with the tire patches, you totally berated me and made *me* feel guilty, when you were the one who got caught stealing.

All my friends had fathers who went to their baseball games, or coached their teams. Some took their sons hunting or fishing or camping. Some were scout leaders. Some dads took their sons to football or baseball or basketball games. You never did anything like that for me. You were just my daddy who I depended on so much and needed so much from, and I was *scared to death of you.* You instilled a fear in me that was so deep I was even afraid to talk to you when we were alone together in the same room. It makes me just want to shake you and wake you up to get your attention and say, "Here I am, Daddy!! Love me!! I'm your son!! You're my daddy, and I don't care that you didn't go to school." I loved you, and I just wanted you to love me. It's not my fault I was different from you. If you compare us now, we don't look so different. Your daddy was an alcoholic, and so was mine. You didn't get the education that you could've gotten and neither did I. Your children were scared of you, and so are mine of me.

You made me feel guilty about things. I lived in fear of what you might do when you were drunk. And I depended on you for my very existence, because Mama didn't work outside of the home.

I was an addict in the making, and there wasn't *thing one* I could do about it then.

You never met my wife and kids, and I used to regret that. I thought that every grandchild should be able to know his grandparents. Well, for my children to have known someone as pathetic as you let yourself become could not have been a pleasant experience for any of us.

I hate what you did to Mama and Sandy and Kathleen and Joe. But I really hate what you did to me. What I wouldn't give for five minutes with you now. I'm not afraid of you anymore. You were just a pathetic old drunk when you died, and you disgust me.

I know it's not written anywhere that life's supposed to be fair, but enough is enough. Just about every aspect of my life is fucked-up in some way or another, and it's all because of your drinking.

When you died I was in the Navy, and everyone thought I should come home for your funeral. As far as I was concerned you had already been dead for two or three years before that.

As far as that goes, I probably would have been better off without a father than I was with a drunk one.

I remember when you used to take us to the Moose Lodge. You used to go in for an hour or two and leave us kids in the car. We'd get rammy after a while and start arguing or fighting with each other, and you'd get mad at us because you had to leave the bar. God, I hated those times. It's strange, because I almost always wanted to go with you, and you pulled that shit almost every time. I must've been starved for your love so much that I'd spend anytime I could with you.

I'm sure I'll think of more instances and things that I'm angry at you about. When I do, I'll send you another letter. But I'll close here for now.

Yours truly,

Phil

## EILEEN'S LETTER TO HUSBAND

Tony,

Because we fight and I cannot express my feelings honestly without being made to feel stupid and confused, I decided to put them on paper. You can read it or not, it's your choice. These are true and honest feelings. You can choose to believe them or not, but they are what I am feeling.

I am a controller! I ran things without anyone's help because I needed to be in control. As a result, you became dependent on me for most things. And I let you. Now that there is help for me, I'm trying not to always be in control. I need to relinquish some of my responsibilities over to you. Only you've gotten too used to having me do it.

And for a while you do try to take over. It infringes on your play time and relaxing time with TV, paper, etc. You resent it! It makes you angry. But you deny those feelings cause you don't want to confront your issues. It's better to make me feel it's all my fault. I'm the problem.

It may be partially true but you are an ACOA and your issues get in the way just as much as mine. Perhaps if you had gone to therapy more or meetings more, you could better understand how I feel. But you're too busy trying to prove how normal you are and fighting the fact that maybe there is something wrong with you. We're not perfect but yet we expect it of ourselves. In that way we don't have to deal with our own character defects.

With the therapy, I'm receiving the conflicting messages of healthy and unhealthy problems and solutions. My emotions are in true turmoil. It's made me rethink all of my choices and decisions. So naturally, I'm concerned and confused over my lifelong commitment to you and the kids. I took a chance with us cause I hoped our love was strong enough. I know how insecure you feel with all this. I also feel insecure. The chance I took I took for me. It's something I needed to do. All I can say is try to roll with it, don't crowd me and try to be understanding and supportive. This may not work out, but it's a chance I had to take in exploring some of my confused feelings.

You need to see me as your equal—not as a maid or convenience to wash your clothes, do your dishes, keep your kids, and occasionally screw. I've made it easy for you to do just that. For years, I've wanted to say just what I felt. But I'm a people pleaser—not an Eileen pleaser. There were times I didn't want to hug and say I love you. But I feared hurting you and displeasing you. I should be able to do and say and think as I feel, not as you feel. And my new independence scares the hell out of you. Pleasing you was a way of not dealing with my own insecurities. The fear of hurting, of not being accepted or loved, the fear of abandonment. So I didn't rock the boat till now.

You need to know I'm fighting for *my* life. I will risk all for the chance to find, love, and nurture me. I will not quit my therapy. I will not accept full responsibility for our problems, and I won't let you think for me any longer. We need to learn to communicate more, share more, and understand more. I may not always say what you want to hear but it'll be honest and they'll be my feelings and not yours or my parents' or anyone else's. If you think you can try to accept me and understand me for who and what I am and need to be, then we have a chance. If not, then I suppose it just wasn't meant to be.

Love,
Eileen

## MARY'S LETTER TO PARENTS

Dear Mom & Dad,

My recovery is very important to me. It's more important than my marriage, my children, my home, or my family. I am fighting for my life in this recovery. I *won't* let anyone or anything get in the way of it. Therefore, since you made a choice to stay unhealthy and I have not, I'm afraid that total detachment from you is necessary. This simply means that I will not be in touch with you in any way or you with me, for at least 1 to 2 years. I know you'll be hurt and angry but no more than I was as a child growing up in an alcoholic home. Please, do not call and ask me to explain detachment to you. If you are confused or need more information, call AA or ACOA. They can direct you to the nearest meetings. But again, it is your choice.

This is not a punishment. I'm simply looking for a healthier way of life for myself and my children. I know you did the best you could with the skills you had. They simply were not enough. I want more! I want healthier children. I want to stop this dreaded disease before it destroys any more of my loved ones. I love you both very much, but I want you to respect my choices as I have come to accept yours.

Love,
Mary

## SUE'S LETTER TO FATHER

Dear Daddy,

I have been pulling back from you because I have been afraid to tell you what I've been going through and working on, afraid of your reaction. However, I need to be honest with you so that sometime in the future, hopefully, we can build a relationship together based on love, respect and appreciation of each other as individuals, rather than one based on my fear of you and my dependency upon you.

I have been in treatment for nearly a year with a therapist who deals almost exclusively with adult children of alcoholics, of whom I am one. I have learned how our family operated, all of us feeding into a very dysfunctional system. I have learned that I never took the opportunity to know what my feelings, needs and values are and to stand up for them. I was too busy trying to please everyone, keeping the peace, and taking care of everyone else. I have learned how Paul and I have, in turn, created a similar dysfunctional family. I want to end the cycle.

I need to learn about me. I need time and space in which to do this. Please respect my request that you not contact me in any way for at least a year. I will contact you again when I am ready to begin building a healthy relationship with you; when I have let go of the old fears and expectations.

Know that I love you. I look forward to developing a strong, healthy relationship with you. If you want more information about adult children of alcoholics (ACOAs) you can contact Alcoholic Anonymous (AA) or Al-Anon.

Love,
Sue

Theme: Confirmation of Self
"GO": Write a welcoming letter to your child or adult. Below are some examples of a client's poems welcoming her total being.

CONNIE'S POEMS ABOUT HER CHILD
Little Package
There is a little girl
she's deep down in.
Very shy and quiet
Doesn't bother to be seen.

No one to have.
No one to hold.
No one to say they care.
This frightened little package
Is filled with despair.

This precious little child
Bring tears to your eyes
Will dance a merry dance
And tickle your insides.

But then you will leave her
Reasons not known why.
But she will survive.
Sometimes she gets so lonely she could die.

But with every little pain
She knows there is a gain.
Though she does not see
What is to see, but the hope is just the same.

So don't be unhappy
And sad you should not feel
For feeling is what gets her through
And you, and you and me!

### Forget-Me-Not

There she is
behind the house.
Why is she hiding?
Why just now?

Hold her for a moment
The smell of sweet perfume,
Gentle as a flower
In the month of June.

Her hair, how it glistens
Her eyes will dance for you
Hold her like a flower
Lest she wither from neglect.

And though you will forget her
This kind and gentle soul
For grasses greener
And pleasures untold.

So question not why she hides
Because you really know
Try to wash away the pain
Like water colors in the rain.

### CONNIE JEAN

You tell me that you like her;
Which one is it you like;
Acting's just a part of her;
So many are inside.

Which one, I ask, which one,
So not to be confused
She plays so many
Past and present, which one.

She speaks of ships passing in the night;
She speaks of sadness down deep inside;
She speaks of love but never found;
She speaks without a sound.

And yet I feel I know her
Though she doesn't let me in.
She's an unkept promise
My wide-eyed wonder,
Connie Jean.

During the transitional time between emergent awareness and core issues, it is beneficial to have the client focus on his/her particular core issues. This also determines the direction of the therapy. A "GO" at this time is to have the client do a collage of his/her core issues. These collages can be left to the creativity of the client. We have received a variety of collages, some of them being words only, pictures only, paintings, etc. This exercise does many things:

- It encourages the client to begin to focus, rather than dealing with many generalizations from the awareness phase.

- it identifies what are the client's particular issues.

- it allows the client to begin to own these issues.

- it develops a readiness to work on these issues.

# Third Stage—Core Issues

The third stage of therapy, working on core issues, helps the client to connect the influence of his/her past with the present, by returning to the past and reliving the relevant experiences. Certain behaviors developed in the past are so pervasive that they appear to be personality traits.

Some of these core issues are: control; difficulty with trust; avoidance of feelings; over-responsibility; denial of personal needs; all-or-nothing functioning; spontaneous age regression, confusion of feeling states; creating and maintaining crises; and low self-esteem. Situations which trigger these issues include those involving trust, flexibility, spontaneity, and sharing (Gravitz/Bowden, 1985).

When clients are in therapy and becoming more aware of their adult-child issues, they tend to become hypersensitive and their feelings fluctuate rapidly. It is important for the therapist to let the client know this fluctuation may/ and probably will, happen. By talking with the client, s/he will be more prepared for changes. A client's becoming aware of his/her past history and taking on the reality of it may cause him/her to become depressed, withdrawn, anxious, etc. (if s/he is not already experiencing these feelings).

The therapist must be aware of the fragility of the client at this stage; thus, this is a logical point at which to introduce the suicide contract. (Although it can be initiated at any time it seems necessary, the timing generally seems most appropriate during the emergent awareness stage or the core issues stage.) The suicide contract is a very powerful tool to protect the client, and also to allow the client to commit to his/her own recovery, well-being and self-caring. Although it is called a "suicide contract," what this tool does is to provide to the client a conscious, self-caring technique that s/he previously was not aware of, did not have skills to perform, or did not give her/himself permission to use.

The suicide contract is taken from the transactional analysis therapy model and is made by the client to him/herself. S/he repeats it at least once daily (or as often during the day as needed). The contract can be made for any length of time, although during the early stages of therapy, we recommend doing it from session to session, with the making of a new contract one of the first items on each session's agenda.

Presenting the suicide contract to the client takes much sensitivity in terms of skill, timing, and allowing enough time to complete the entire contract process during the session. The therapist must also realize that the client may either be resistant to the contract or feel he/she has no reason to be making such a contract—in which case s/he may be put off by such a suggestion.

The four clauses of the suicide contract are as follows:

1. From now until *(next session)* (the amount of time contract is good for) I will not intentionally or accidentally hurt or kill myself.

2. From now until *(next session)*, I will not intentially or accidentally hurt or kill someone else.

3. From now until *(next session)*, I will not intentionally or accidentally set myself up to be hurt or killed.

4. From now until (next session), I will not go crazy.

The therapist takes one statement at a time and has the client repeat it until the client sounds convincing and sure of the commitment to each statement.

In many cases, clients have difficulty with a particular statement. Indications of this include:

- forgetting words or complete statements

- laughing

- hyperventilating

- general confusion.

The therapist can use the situation as an opportunity to explore with the client his/her feelings in connection with the particular statement in the contract. Many clients have reported that making the contract, put them in touch with their self-destructive actions and thoughts for the first time. They had never before linked many of their normal ways of living with non-caring or destructive behavior.

After introducing all four statements individually, the client then repeats the entire contract. It is helpful for the client to repeat the contract to someone else in the office, or to him/herself in a mirror.

Doing this contract many times allows the client and therapist to be aware of areas of difficulty and/or vulnerability. If, for example, the client reports not being able to remember certain parts, or s/he omits particular words, the therapist should consider these actions as "red flags" indicating places where the client may not be self-caring.

As the client continues journal writing and reading during the core-issues stage, s/he also requires very intensive therapy with support (ACOA and Al-Anon) groups to work through the various issues. This can be accomplished in many ways and with many different therapeutic techniques.

Another helpful component of treatment at this stage is hypnotherapy, which the therapist can use to facilitate age regression for the client. Herb Gravitz believes that ACOAs may be continually in trance or capable of being in trance at anytime. We feel that is very true and that clients are in trance much of the time in treatment. Using trance and hypnosis (one and the same thing, in our opinion) can allow the client to safely visit situations from his/her childhood and reparent that child with new healthy messages and belief systems. Teaching the client self-hypnosis provides a tool with which s/he can create—and feel capable of creating—his/her own safe space at any time.

In teaching the client self-hypnosis, we use many relaxation techniques, including visualization, to provide him/her a variety of ways to deal with stress, whether internally or externally provoked. Relaxation plays many important roles during the entire therapy. From almost the beginning of therapy, the client has relaxation "GOs" that lead up to his/her giving him/herself permission to play (a lost art for ACOAs).

Work with the "inner child," "the child," "the child within," or whatever name one prefers, is a very important part of the core issues stage and of the integration of the client as an adult. Using trance and hypnosis is very helpful in bringing the client into contact with his/her child. "GOs" given at this point can help the client and child. Below is an example of a client exploring his child and recognizing the need for that part of the person (the child) to be an integral part of him.

To Luke Skywalker
 c/o Yoda
 The Degobah Star System

Dear Jimmy,
  I know that I told Rose and Jane that your nickname is Luke Skywalker, but you and I both know what your real name is.

I understand that your real daddy didn't fulfill a lot of the needs that you have, and that he rejected you, because he felt threatened by your intelligence. These things aren't your fault, and they weren't your daddy's fault either. You see, Jimmy, your daddy was a very sick man. He didn't love himself, so it was impossible for him to love you. He simply could not give you what he didn't have.

OK now, where does that leave you? That leaves you stuck with all these unfulfilled needs. That's where I come in. Actually, I've always been here physically, but not spiritually. I didn't love myself very much either, but that's changing rapidly. The more I love myself, the more ready and willing I am to take over the care and responsibility of you.

I love you, Jimmy, just because you are who you are, and I am here to take care of you and help you grow up to become a responsible, feeling, loving, caring, and strong young man.

I can feel your doubts, and hey, I don't blame you one bit. If I was in your shoes I'd be wary also. After 34 years of not being there for you, I'm now asking you to believe that I'm here for you now, and I always will be.

I promise that I won't neglect you, and that I'll always be here to take care of your needs. I know that you don't fully believe these words yet, but I do know that you like what you've seen so far. If you will trust me, and let me take care of you, I believe you'll find more of the same.

Once again, Jimmy, I promise that I shall always be here for you, and I shall always take care of you and see to it that your needs are met.

So Hello Jimmy!! You'll never be alone again. Because I'll always be here for you. And I am the only one who will always be here for you.

I love you, Jimmy!!

Love,
Jim

Besides hypnosis to deal with the child in the client, we also use the Gestalt method of the empty chair for resolving unfinished or unresolved relationships that the client may have. This is particularly useful when the relationship and/or other person is particularly threatening or unavailable. In many cases, clients need to practice how they will approach another person, or need to see how that other person has affected him/herself. The empty chair can facilitate this greatly.

"GOs" are an integral piece of the therapy during the resolution of core issues. They can be assigned to help the client as various therapeutic issues surface, assisting him/her in everything from developing his/her awareness about the issue to creating and integrating self-decisions about how to change behavior around that issue.

An additional therapeutic tool for this stage of therapy or a later stage is the family reconstruction (now termed restoration) developed by Virginia Satir. The restoration process provides a highly experimental, intensive therapeutic regimen that allows participants to thoroughly explore their own families of origin and confront the impact of familial alcoholism. In essence, the experience is designed to give participants a new foundation for choice (Miller, 1985).

There are various restoration workshops offered throughout the country. Trained therapists guide a "star" or key recovering person through a complicated day long reconstruction of his/her family experiences. In this process individuals from the group of ACOA participants play members of the "star's" family. This enables them to get in touch with many of their own family of origin issues and through therapeutic processes begin or continue their recovery. Among the therapeutic processes is a technique referred to as family sculpturing. Clients actually use other group participants to act out or sculpture simple family scenes remembered from the past. Many feelings evolve from this dramatization and oftentimes the client is able to express previously submerged feelings to the pseudo-family members. Through the reconstruction and sculpturing processes many long term conflicts and misunderstandings can be resolved or at least surfaced for future resolution by the client.

The technique of sculpturing is also a valuable tool in an office group therapy setting. Clients are able to use other members of the group as family members or friends to work through various issues. The restoration workshop and group therapy setting provide "safe" environments in which the client can work through difficult family confrontations.

During the core issues stage, we generally employ a combination of individual and group therapy. Timing is a very important factor in considering when clients are prepared for group therapy. The client must have first established a trusting relationship with the therapist in individual therapy before being considered for group. Trust is generally a core issue for ACOAs since their pasts are filled with broken promises and delusions. Therefore, if clients have not established trust with at least one person (the therapist) before beginning group, they would be unable to extend themselves completely to establish healthy relationships with others.

Under the condition of a trust relationship with the therapist and with the proper timing, group therapy is a most effective treatment modality for ACOAs. It is reassuring for a client to learn that s/he is not the only person who had particular experiences and feelings about family situations. Group therapy provides an experiential environment for clients to learn and practice new functional adult behavior with other ACOAs under the guidance of a professional therapist.

The operating concept for group therapy sessions dealing with core issues is somewhat different from that normally at work in regular personal-growth groups. In fact, these sessions are actually individual therapy within a group setting. The therapist, while working on a particular issue with a client or clients, encourages the other group members to change the script to fit their own situations. What this means for the client is that his/her primary attention is on him/herself; the support s/he receives from or gives to others in the group is secondary.

The group is structured this way for several reasons. While many issues are basic to all clients, each client has his/her individual history concerning any particular issue; by changing the script to his/her own situation, s/he can benefit directly even while the therapist's focus is on someone else. (This makes the group session an economical use of the client's time.) The structure minimizes opportunities to rely on enabling, a behavior clients are likely to want to use in a group, especially if they are anxious about the situation. It also removes the opportunity for clients to assume the role of caretaker—a role that many ACOAs have played all their lives, and that they would fall into automatically if support were the primary concern of the group. The focus on self makes it possible that individuals will receive self-validation; they may also receive validation from the group.

For many clients, group therapy also is the first experience of a healthy family (or multiple-member) system. Because they have been raised in an unhealthy or dysfunctional environment, they tend to gravitate toward those kinds of systems in their work environment and also recreate that unhealthiness in their own family. They are encouraged to see the group as a laboratory where they can experiment with healthy relations and try behaviors that might otherwise be unacceptable in their other environs. If two therapists are working with a group of six to ten clients, for example, this laboratory system can be well monitored.

We offer our clients a sequence of two different types of groups: the "awareness group" and the "core issues group." In the awareness group, we review and reinforce many of the emergent awareness issues. Clients in this group may not have much information about the alcoholic family system and its effect on them as adults; for this reason, the group is primarily educational and structured, using a variety of instructional materials. While the sophistication of the material we use varies according to the general awareness level of the clients participating, our main focus remains the same: education and preparation for the core issues group.

A sample agenda for an awareness group in which clients have limited knowledge of ACOA issues follows:

Week One:   — Group begins with introduction/ warmup activity.
— Discussion of the need not to drink during treatment and perhaps forever because codependents are a high risk for alcoholism.
— Hand out list of group members and phone numbers for support calls.
— List of community resources, such as lectures and support meetings, of interest to ACOAs.
— Basic awareness articles on ACOA is-

sues, such as fear of crying, control feelings and faulty thinking.
— Show film of "Velveteen Rabbit" to illustrate the meaning of "What Is Real?"

Week Two:    — Discussion on relaxation and practice on breathing.
— Teach journal-writing structure.
— Expose clients to various books helpful for the recovery process.
— Discussion of the roles in an alcoholic family system and having clients identify the roles they played in the past and present.

Week Three:  — Film "Soft Is the Heart of a Child" used to show an alcoholic family, roles played, and possible intervention method.
— Teach how to give self-affirmations.

Week Four:   — Teach concepts of detachment and enabling.
— Film "Tale of O" used to illustrate being different.

Week Five:   — Define core issues.
— Clients make collages of their own individual core issues and share with group.
— Film "Twelve Steps" used to familiarize clients with the twelve steps of recovery.

Week Six:    — Explain concept of core issues group.
— Clients from core issues group share

personal experience with awareness group.
— Discussion of commitment to group and process of leaving group.

Once a client has completed the awareness group series, s/he is ready for the core issues group. The core issues group does not have the education-oriented structure of the awareness group; rather, clients come prepared to work on a particular issue. An individual client contracts for six sessions of the core issues group. At the end of each six sessions, the client meets with his/her therapist to determine whether or not s/he should continue in the core issues group and to define the issues still to be worked. When the client determines to continue in another six sessions, s/he writes a contract to him/herself stating s/he will complete the series. ACOAs many times do not know how to leave situations that are uncomfortable, and without a contract they may just leave the group without any notice to the group.

At the completion of six or twelve sessions, a marathon group is conducted. The marathon is either a one-day or a two-day event, including group therapy and sessions focusing on particular issues of interest identified by the clients. Play is also an important part of the marathon.

The therapists in the core issues group choose from the techniques already mentioned (confronting, empty chair, hypnosis, role playing, etc.) according to the issues with which the group is dealing. Having two therapists present allows for a variety of therapeutic methods to be used. It also allows the therapists to model for the clients examples of healthy interactions between two people.

The client is given the responsiblity to bring to group the issue(s) that s/he wants to work on. The issue may be one s/he is working on in individual therapy, or something that is possibly given to him/her by the individual therapist as a "GO" to explore or resolve in the group. At the end of each core issues group, each client receives an evaluation form to fill out for the next session. It is then the client's responsibility to evaluate his/her participation, or lack of it, in the group—something the client may find valuable to work on in the next session. The evaluation is found in Exhibit 6.

## EXHIBIT 6

### SELF-EVALUATION FOR ACOA GROUP

1. Was I honest with group members about what I saw in their behavior? If yes, how? If no, why not?
2. Was I honest with group members abut how I felt toward them? If yes, how? If no, why not?
3. How did I let people into my life during group? If I did not, why not?
4. What emotions did I identify during group?
5. What emotions did I express directly during group?
6. Did I use telling a story, giving an analysis, saying I don't know, or questions of clarification to hide what I was really feeling?
7. When was I afraid to share my feelings?
8. What defenses did I use during group?
9. What risks did I take?
10. What was I afraid to look at during group?
11. What am I most proud of about myself during group?
12. What are my goals for the next group?

Reprinted with permission from *Tumbleweeds* by Paul Curtin.

Published by Quotidian Publishers, Delaware Water Gap, PA.

# Fourth Stage—Transformations

After confronting the various core issues, the client is ready to make changes in his/her behavior and life and begin the fourth stage, transformations. "As core issues are identified, more of the behaviors of adult children can be seen in the context necessary to change them. Meaning can be found and connections made. Only then can choice and freedom be discovered" (Gravitz/Bowden, 1985). Specific workshops on various behaviors, such as communications, assertiveness, and decision making, are appropriate to give the client a more secure feeling in handling the various issues as an adult.

Because groups are extremely effective with these clients, the adult child should continue to participate in an ACOA psychotherapeutic group. This will enable him/her to continue working on the various adult children issues and, because of the group structure, will help him/her begin to focus on relationship issues.

The therapist must be aware of the difficulty that the client might be having with one or more particular core issues. An additional therapeutic tool to help the client come to some resolution about these issues is the ordeal, described by Jay Haley in *Ordeal Therapy*. Ordeals can help the adult child break a cycle of the compulsive behavior. "With the ordeal technique, the therapist's task is easily defined: It is to impose an ordeal appropriate to the problem (compulsion) of the client. The ordeal must be more severe than the problem and cause distress equal to or greater than that caused by the symptoms" (Haley, 1984).

Ordeals can be useful at various stages of recovery but

seem most appropriate during the transformation stage. It is at this time in the recovery that the client is very aware of a particular issue but may be having a tremendous amount of difficulty changing the behavior. A few reasons for this difficulty may be the status and safety the behavior provided in the past (especially during childhood), the habitual nature of the behavior, or the fear of the unknown the new behavior creates. The therapist must be very clever in creating an ordeal that addresses the issues at hand and provides enough discomfort that the client will choose the new behavior rather than continuing old patterns.

The following example is an ordeal that emphasized the core issues with which the client was experiencing difficulty and also was distasteful enough to perform the ordeal that the client chose to take charge of himself.

The predominant core issue of this male client was the use of money (i.e., control). During a particular period of therapy, the client was having tremendous difficulty taking on his control (and blame) issue and would invariably blame (dump) particular situations (especially money-oriented) on his wife and strike out at his kids. The object of the ordeal was to encourage the client to own his behavior and feelings involving control and money issues. Generally his feelings centered on his not having enough money (which was not true) or wanting to have total control of the money within the family. (To understand the full effect of the ordeal, one must know that the client had two alcoholic parents, lived in a surburban area about thirty miles from a city where he worked, and drove to his work daily.)

The ordeal was to take place in the following manner whenever the client blamed (dumped on) his wife or children for various money situations. The night following the "dumping," the client was to go to bed at his regular time, set his alarm for 3 A.M., get up, go to the nearest automatic teller machine and withdraw $50.00 in cash, drive to the city where he worked, find a street man (known in Philadelphia as a vent man), give him the cash without preaching to him about how he should use it, and then drive home. At home he was to write in his journal about the "dumping" and the ordeal, and make a plan to own his behavior, then go back to bed until the morning. The difficulty of the ordeal was having to get up in the middle of the night, driving a long distance that he did everyday (certainly not wanting to repeat it anymore than necessary), giving money away without just cause, dealing with an alcoholic person and not controlling the person in telling him how he should spend the money. After two experiences with having to do the ordeal, the client finally broke through the barrier of blaming and dumping and began to take on his control issue by taking charge of his behavior, providing a plan for himself, and following it!!

During the transformation process of the ACOA from child to adult, the therapist needs to be aware of the importance of practice time for the client. The ACOA will spend much time during this stage experiencing new behaviors and skills, so therapeutic sessions should be scheduled to allow him/her enough time between appointments to become acquainted with these newly acquired skills, and begin to incorporate them into their adult being.

# Fifth Stage—Integration

Once these practiced skills become more comfortable to the ACOA, s/he moves to the fifth stage, integration. This stage occurs as the adult child accepts and addresses both the negative and positive aspects of his/her life and allows him/her to make all parts of the self available to him/herself. During integration, the ACOA acquires choice over his/her behavior and learns motivation. The thinking, feeling and doing of the adult child become one and the same. As the fanatical need to control and all-or-nothing functioning disappear, s/he sets appropriate limits with self and others, and establishes open and trusting relationships, and begins to play. The ACOA may not have learned how to have sober fun (if s/he was alcoholic) or how to have fun at all ( if s/he functioned as the parent in his/her family of origin and therefore is forever vigilant). Play can be incorporated in the client's daily routine—as can doing something for him/herself each day, as suggested by Colgrove, et al. in *How to Survive the Loss of a Love.*

The therapist must help the adult child to guard against becoming a so-called "intensity junkie" (Smith, 1985), who, because of his/her frantic use of all of the tools, feels that the activity of therapy is synonymous with the illusive dreams of "being recovered." The therapist must encourage the client to integrate the therapy into his/her life rather than let the therapy become his/her life. This ensures that the focus for the adult child is on recovery as a complete person, not on participation in various therapeutic processes.

During this integration stage, the adult child assumes a

67

new responsibility for self, and takes charge of the often unfriendly, critical gremlin on the shoulder, and continues to nurture his/her new adult self. Like alcoholics, adult children need to accept that their history will always be a part of them, but also to be aware that through therapy they have developed new skills to live more positively and completely.

At this point in therapy (if not before), it may be appropriate to focus on family treatment, since the locked-family system (resulting from the disease and its aftermath) commonly retards the growth of the client (LaBundy, 1985). When working with the ACOA's family, the therapist must be sure to work with diads, then triads, etc., rather than trying to work with the entire family.

The therapist may also choose to refer the family to a treatment center that specializes in alcoholic family recovery. An example of this is the Caron Foundation in Wernersville, Pa., which offers a five-day residental program. One parent and one child participate in the program, living in a larger group of about twelve people. Much of the emphasis is on identifying roles, sculpturing the family, and participating in a variety of group compositions (adults, children, and mixed).

During this time of integration, the client is taking charge of providing a healthy adult life for him/herself. This may include a number of areas in the client's life—work, relationships, family, play, and balance of life in general. One way of starting anew in a relationship that the client has been in is a renewal of marriage vows. Clients find this to be much more of a real commitment than the original ceremony and vows. An example of a client's renewal of vows follows.

VOWS

I, Doug, take you, Betty, to be my equal partner in marriage. As your partner in marriage, I shall share parts of me with you that I'll share with no one else. I shall treat you with respect, and kindness, and I shall work hard to do my part to ensure that we both get the time and space we need to grow. I sincerely hope that our relationship will remain special through our lifetime, but I realize that only God knows what lies in the future for us; so I am content in the knowledge that we are together today. Today, I give you all the love that I don't need for me.

Another part of the integration stage is the beginning of spirituality. By recognizing and accepting the disease in his/her life, the ACOA uses it as a springboard to recovery. That is spirituality. In the surrender —i.e., the admittance of the disease in his/her life—is the beginning of recovery. Al-Anon, Alateen, and ACOA have all discovered that the key to recovery and spiritual growth can only begin with the rigorously honest awareness of how the disease has touched the adult child's life. The anger, resentments, feelings of abandonment, and loneliness can only be healed through the awareness and expression of these feelings. Real pain does not simply disappear—that would be magic. Spiritual growth blossoms in ACOAs' lives when they take responsibility for the disease and begin to understand and live with it.

# Sixth Stage—Genesis

Through the process of maturation gained from the first five stages, the emerging adult enters the final stage, Genesis. This stage, truly a beginning for the adult child, is analogous to the "spiritual awakening" spoken of in AA. "Unlike integration, in which there develops a congruency among the different parts of self, Genesis involves a synergistic relationship greater than the sum of those separate parts. This expansion of self can be characterized by the development of personal, specific, powerful, and enduring relationship with a higher power or higher self. Guidance, strength, and nourishment begin to flow from this relationship. Also with this relationship comes a fundamental change in perception of reality" (Gravitz/Bowden, 1985).

The spiritual program for an ACOA is an effort to discover a higher power in his/her life. S/he begins to understand the freedom and beauty of being an individual in his/her own right. A true love of a higher power and self is practiced in:

- being able to get in touch with and express feelings,

- being able to trust and take risks in their lives,

- creating and sustaining relationships (Booth, 1985).

A journal entry that a client wrote during the emergence of her Genesis stage follows below.

Hi Tammy,

How are you; I feel very spiritual; I am praying for God to remove my self centered fears, so I may be his servant and to do his will only and always. I feel I am at a turning point. I truly

71

believe in my Higher Power—his power is of a capacity I can only feel within myself. I cannot explain it, I pray only to bear witness to my God's power, love and way of life. I felt a spiritual awakening this morning, I felt my body as not being mine, I am only borrowing it, I am of spirit, God is in me and I am his servant, to go forth and do his bidding. This space I am in is needed here on earth, because people are made of flesh and blood but that is only external, my force is from within. I in body am needed to voice and express the journey of the reason for being.

I have abandoned self, so that I can speak honestly of my God and be of use to him and my fellows. I am on a mission for the will of the power greater than me. I am only human and could not encompass something so grand as God's reasoning for his work. I need not question why; it doesn't matter. I will first do what God wills for me. I feel very different today. I feel very new, and refreshed, full, touched.

I pray for God's will always!

> I love you, Tammy, and
> commit to this way of life.
> Tammy

With a new and highly developed sense of self and an enduring relationship with a higher power, the client is able to enter into meaningful adult relationships. The therapist can help the client to begin to look outside of self and be attuned to the needs of others. This will then complete the circle of integrating the *I, me,* and *we* stages of recovery.

"Genesis seems to require a program of prayer and/or meditation coupled with a variety of other health-enhancing practices. It is important to give this new lifestyle an ongoing, conscious commitment. In Genesis, there is true forgiveness and love. Serenity becomes the predominant feeling" (Gravitz/Bowden, 1985).

In most cases, adult-child therapy is completed before

the beginning of the sixth stage, having allowed the healing of the child and the emergence of an adult living in the present. Still, from time to time during this new adult's life, various interventions by the therapist may help him/her deal with issues of the present day. Genesis provides for an ongoing expansion of self and the continuing growth of the adult. In Genesis, the adult child becomes his/her own therapist.

# Conclusion—A New Beginning

Gravitz and Bowden have given the sixth and final stage of therapy for the adult child a particularly apt name: They call it Genesis—life from lifelessness. As the adult child encounters all six stages of therapy, his/her adult life begins to awaken and becomes meaningful. For the therapist, even though providing therapy for clients with adult-children issues is very demanding, it is a privilege to observe (and experience) the client creating a new beginning: evolving from a closed, lifeless period of survival to an open, beautiful creation of a loving being, full of life.

Virginia Satir, in *Meditations and Inspirations* (1985), describes the new life of the adult child in the following poem.

## A NEW PRESENT

It is the human situation to meet the present with interpretations of the past.

The meaning of the present is to allow us to leave the past and see the Now in its own right.

Experience will soon become your past and a foundation for a new present and future.

The suggested reading is presented here as information for therapists. Therapists need to regularly update their information since new terrain is continually being charted in the study of ACOAs.

# Suggested Reading

Ackerman, Robert. *Children of Alcoholics*. Holmes Beach: Learning Publications, 1978.

Alberti, Robert E., Ph.D. and Michael L. Emmons, Ph.D. *Your Perfect Right*. San Luis Obispo: Impact Publishers, 1982.

Black, Claudia, M.S.W., Ph.D. *It Will Never Happen to Me*. Denver: M.A.C. Printing & Publications Division, 1985.

Booth, Reverend Leonard. *Alcoholism: A Problem Exposed*. Long Beach: Emmaus Limited, 1983.

Carter, Elizabeth A., A.C.S.W. and Monica McGoldrick, A.C.S.W., ed. *The Family Cycle*. New York: Gardner Press, Inc., 1980.

Cruse, Joseph R., M.D. *The Romance: A Story of Chemical Dependency*. St. Paul: Nurturing Networks, Inc., 1985.

Curtin, Paul J., M.A., C.A.C. *Tumbleweeds: A Therapist's Guide to Treatment of ACOA's*. Stroudsburg: Quotidian, 1985.

Curtin, Paul J., M.A., C.A.C. *Resistance and Recovery for Adult Children of Alcoholics*. Delaware Water Gap: Quotidian, 1987.

Deutsch, Charles. *Broken Bottles, Broken Dreams*. New York: Teachers College Press, 1982.

Finnegan, Dana G., Ph.D., CAC and Emily B. McNally, M.Ed., CAC. *Dual Identities*. Minneapolis: Hazeldon Educational Materials, 1987.

Grateful Members. *The Twelve Steps for Everyone*. Minneapolis: CompCare Publications, 1985.

Gravitz, Herbert L. and Julie D. Bowden. *Guide to Recovery: A Book for Adult Children of Alcoholics*. Holmes Beach: Learning Publications, Inc., 1985.

Gravitz, Herbert and Julie D. Bowden. *Genesis: Spritituality in Recovery from Childhood Traumas*. Pompano Beach: Health Communications, Inc., 1988.

Hajcak, Frank, Ph.D. and Patricia Garwood, M.S. *Hidden Bedroom Partners*. San Diego: Libra Publishers, Inc., 1987.

Haley, Jay. *Ordeal Therapy*. Washington: Jossey-Bass Publishers, 1984.

James, Muriel, Ed.D., and Dorothy Jongeward, Ph.D. *Born to Win*. Reading: Addison-Wesley Publishing Co., Inc., 1971.

Kaufman, Gershen. *Shame.* Cambridge: Schenkman Publishing Company, Inc., 1980.

Kempe, Ruth S. and C. Henry. *The Common Secret.* New York: W.H. Freeman and Company, 1984.

Leite, Evelyn, *Detachment.* Minneapolis: Johnson Institute, Inc., 1980.

Little, Bill L. *This Will Drive You Sane.* Minneapolis: CompCare Publications, 1977.

Martin, Father C. *No Laughing Matter.* Philadelphia: Harper & Row Publishers, 1977.

Maxwell, Ruth. *The Booze Battle.* New York: Praeger Publishers, Inc., 1976.

O'Gorman, Patricia and Philip Oliver-Diaz. *Breaking The Cycle of Addiction.* Pompano Beach: Health Communications, Inc., 1987.

Satir, Virginia. *Your Many Faces.* Berkeley: Celestial Arts, 1978.

Schaef, Anne Wilson. *When Society Becomes an Addict.* San Franciso: Harper & Row Publishers, 1987.

Smith, Ann W. *Grandchildren of Alcoholics.* Pompano Beach: Health Communications, Inc., 1988.

Steiner, Claude, Ph.D. *Games Alcoholics Play.* New York: Ballantine Books, 1971.

Stevens, John O. *Awareness.* Moab: Real People Press, 1971.

Twerski, Abraham, J., M.D. *Caution: Kindness Can Be Dangerous to the Alcoholic.* Englewood Cliffs: Prentice-Hall, Inc., 1981.

Twerski, Abraham, J., M.D. *Like Yourself & Others Will, Too.* Englewood Cliffs: Prentice-Hall, Inc., 1978.

Twerski, Abraham, J., M.D. *Self Discovery in Recovery.* Minneapolis: Hazeldon Educational Materials, 1984.

Wegscheider, Sharon. *Another Chance.* Palo Alto: Science & Behavior Books, Inc., 1981.

Wegscheider, Sharon. *Co-Dependency.* St. Paul: Nurturing Networks. Inc., 1984.

Wegscheider, Sharon. *Family Freedom.* St. Paul: Nurturing Networks. Inc., 1980.

Wegscheider, Sharon. *Making Choices.* St. Paul: Nurturing Networks, Inc., 1983.

Wegscheider, Sharon. *Ongoing Recovery.* St. Paul: Nurturing Networks, Inc., 1985.

Wegscheider, Sharon. *Recover or Repeat.* St. Paul: Nurturing Networks, Inc., 1982.

Wegscheider, Sharon. *The Family Trap*. St. Paul: Nurturing Networks, Inc., 1976.

Wegscheider, Sharon. *The Hidden Illness*. St. Paul: Nurturing Networks, Inc., 1983.

Wegscheider, Sharon, and Marty Becker. *The Intervention*. St. Paul: Nurturing Networks, Inc., 1982.

Wegscheider-Cruse, Sharon. *Choicemaking*. Pompano Beach: Health Communications, Inc., 1985.

Wegscheider-Cruse, Sharon. *Understanding Me*. Pompano Beach: Health Communications, Inc., 1985.

Weinstein, Matt and Joel Goodman. *Playfair*. San Luis Obispo: Impact Publishers, 1980.

Whitfield, Charles, L., M.D. *Healing the Child Within*. Baltimore: The Resource Group, 1986.

Woititz, Janet. *Adult Children of Alcoholics*. Hollywood: Health Communications, Inc., 1983.

Woititz, Janet. *Struggle for Intimacy*. Pompano Beach: Health Communications, Inc., 1985.

*Alcoholics Anonymous*. New York: Alcoholics Anonymous World Services, Inc., 1976.

# Articles

Balls, Susan A., M.S.S. "Illustrations that Affect Treatment." *Focus on Family*, May/June, 1985, pp. 16–17, 33.

Booth, Father Leo. "Spirituality for the Family & Adult Children of Alcoholics." *Focus on Family*, September/October, 1985, pp. 31–32.

Friel, John C., Ph.D. "Co-Dependency Assessment Inventory." *Focus on Family*, May/June, 1985, pp. 21–22.

Friesen, Victor I. and Nancy T. Casella. "The Rescuing Therapist: A Duplication of the Pathogenic Family System." *The American Journal of Family Therapy*, Winter, 1982, Vol. 10, No. 4, pp. 57–61.

Gravitz, Herbert L., Ph.D. and Julie D. Bowden, M.S. "Recovery Continuum for Adult Children of Alcoholics." *Focus on Family*, May/June 1985, pp. 6–7, 39–40.

Howland, Vaughan J. "The Invisible Problem." *Networker*, November/December, 1985, pp. 15–16.

LaBundy, James F., M.S., C.A.C. "Simulating Family Bonding." *Focus on Family*, September/October, 1985, pp. 22–23, 39.

Leiken, Celia. "Identifying and Treating the Alcoholic Client." *Social Casework: The Journal of Contemporary Social Work*, February, 1986, pp. 67–73.

McKenna, Thomas and Roy Pickens. "Personality Characteristics of Adult Children of Alcoholics." *Journal of Studies On Alcohol*, July, 1983, Vol. 44, No. 4, pp. 688–700.

McKenna, Thomas and Roy Pickens. "Adult Children of Alcoholics." *Journal of Studies on Alcohol*, March, 1981, Vol. 42, No. 11, pp. 1021–1029.

Miller, Michael E., M.S., C.A.C. "Reconstruction: Creating Opportunity for Choice." *Focus on Family*, September/October, pp. 52–53.

Neuhausel, Patricia. "Alone in a Crowd: Lack of Help for a Family with a Learning Disabled Child." Bryn Mawr College, November, 1984.

Neuhausel, Patricia. "Neuhausel-Garvin Alcoholic Genogram Study." Bryn Mawr College, February, 1985.

Neuhausel, Patricia. "Family Dynamics of Adult Child of Alcoholic Family." Bryn Mawr College, April, 1985.

Policoff, Stephen Phillip. "Bottle Babies." *New Age*, October, 1985, pp. 54–60.

Smith, Ann W., M.S., C.A.C. "Treatment Issues for Addicted Adult Children from Alcoholic Families." *Focus on Family*, March/April, 1985.

Stuckey, Robert F. "Daughters of Alcoholics and the Women's Movement." *Focus on Family*, May/June, 1985, pp. 30–31, 37.

Treadway, David, Ph.D. "Who's on First?" *Focus on Family*, September/ October, 1985, pp. 14–15, 34–35.

Worden, Mark. "Family as Patient: Implications of a Paradigm Shift." *Focus on Family*, September/October, 1985, pp. 6–7, 46.

Youcha, Geraldine, and Judith Seixas. "The Longest Hangover." *Philadelphia*, April, 1985, pp. 93–97.

Wegscheider, Sharon. "From 'Reconstruction' to 'Restoration'." *Focus on Family*, September/October, 1983, pp. 9–10.

# Tapes

Bloomfield, Harold H., M.D. *Making Peace with Your Parents.* Listen & Learn USA, ISBN No. 0-88684-020-1Y.

Bowden, Julie, M.S. *Guide to Recovery for Adult Children of Alcoholics and Professionals.* U.C.L.A., 7/18/86.

Gravitz, Herbert, Ph.D. *Recovery for Adult Children of Alcoholics.* Custom Cassettes, Port Allegany, Pa., 16743.

Wegscheider, Sharon. *Co-Dependency.* Nurturing Networks.

Wegscheider, Sharon. *Children of Alcoholics.* Nuturing Networks.

Wegscheider, Sharon. *Hidden Illness.* Nuturing Networks.

Wegscheider, Sharon. *Making Choices.* Nuturing Networks.

Wegscheider, Sharon. *Family Aftercare & Recovery.* Nuturing Networks.

Wegscheider, Sharon. *The Alcoholic American Family Challenges the Professional Family.* Nuturing Networks.

# Lectures

Crandall, Patsy. "My Family, Your Family: Addiction Across the Generations." The Sixth Annual Training Institute on Addictions, Clearwater Beach, 9 Feb., 1985.

Neuhausel, Patricia. "Identification and General Intervention of Adult Children of Alcoholics." ToughLove Meeting. Exton, 9 May, 1985.

Wegscheider-Cruse, Sharon. "Roles in the Alcoholic Family." The Sixth Annual Training Institute on Addictions, Clearwater Beach, 8 Feb., 1985.

Zawadski, Mary Lee. "The Adult Child of the Alcoholic." The Sixth Annual Training Institute on Addictions, Clearwater Beach, 10 Feb., 1985.

Zawadski, Mary Lee. "Recovery Process for the Adult Child." The Sixth Annual Training Institute on Addictions, Clearwater Beach, 10 Feb., 1985.

# About the Authors

Patricia Mansmann is a leading therapist, educator and lecturer in the drug and alcohol field. Twenty years of experience with a primary focus on adolescents has enabled Pat to become a national and international presenter of seminars and workshops. The many personally created seminars include such subjects as parenting, essence of love, stress, drugs and alcohol, and alcoholic family systems.

Pat received her master's degree in counseling from Duquesne University, is a Pennsylvania Certified Addictions Counselor (CAC) and has worked with Crisis Intervention in Chester County for many years. She is the co-director of Genesis Associates in Exton, PA, a private practice specializing in adult children of alcoholics, addictions and wellness. As a part of her extensive experience with adolescents she has been a Prevention Specialist in several school systems as well as being the developer of Student Assistance Programs.

Patricia Neuhausel is a prominant therapist, educator and discussion leader in the field of addictions with particular emphasis on adult children of alcoholics. As a clinical social worker with a M.S.S. degree from Bryn Mawr College, Pat has become a national and international presenter of seminars and workshops on such topics as alcoholism, addictive family systems, and sexuality. She is also a Pennsylvania Certified Addictions Counselor (CAC). Pat is co-director of Genesis Associates in Exton, PA, a private practice specializing in addictions, adult children of alcoholics, and wellness.

In preparation for her profession as a therapist, Pat pursued many fields of endeavor including: AMS certification as a Montessori instructor; relocation consultant with a major corporation; drug and alcohol consultant for adolescents; and therapeutic support for corporate and union employee assistance programs.

Pat and Pat are creative therapists who are continually developing innovative methods to treat adult children of alcoholics. "Pats' People," the endearing term used by one ACOA to describe their clients, can be easily spotted in a crowd because of their healthy demeanors. The individual and group therapy processes are complementary to each other and fit with the holistic approach offered by Pat and Pat. Sometimes they are referred to as mavericks in the field because of the unique therapeutic techniques that help their clients to grow in recovery.

They are international presenters of a wide variety of topics to groups ranging from the Catholic Church to the National Association of Social Workers.

This second edition of *Life After Survival* is indicative of their growth and their timeless pursuit to treat the most special people of all—adult children of alcoholics.

# NOTES

# NOTES

# NOTES

# LIFE AFTER SURVIVAL :
## A Therapeutic Approach for Adult Children of Alcoholics
## ( 2nd Edition )

**by Patricia A. Mansmann**
**Patricia A. Neuhausel**

**forwards by  Herbert L. Gravitz**
**Julie D. Bowden**

This expanded second edition links together the multifaceted approaches for treating adult children of alcoholics into one concise guide for therapists. This book is also recommended for adult children themselves to enable them to become better therapeutic consumers.  The second edition includes actual examples of clients' work during their therapeutic process.  The authors have used their own experiences and a thorough information gathering to provide therapists with a practical and structural approach to enhance the treatment of adult children of alcoholics.

-------------------------------------------------------------------------------------------------------------

This book may be ordered by sending this form directly to the publishing company:
GENESIS PUBLISHING CO., BOX #228, MALVERN, PA 19355

Please send me _____ copies of **LIFE AFTER SURVIVAL : A Therapeutic Approach for Adult Children of Alcoholics ( 2nd Edition )** at $6.95 plus $2.00 (P/H) per copy to:

_____          _____
Name                                                       Occupation

_____
Address

_____
City                            State                          Zip
Make check payable to : Genesis Publishing Co.